A Robbie Reader

What's So Great About...?

DANIEL BOONE

Russell Roberts

P.O. Box 196
Hockessin, Delaware 19707
Visit us on the web: www.mitchelllane.com
Comments? email us: mitchelllane@mitchelllane.com

Mitchell Lane
PUBLISHERS

Printing   1   2   3   4   5   6   7   8   9

A Robbie Reader/What's So Great About . . . ?

Annie Oakley	**Daniel Boone**	Davy Crockett
Ferdinand Magellan	Francis Scott Key	Henry Hudson
Jacques Cartier	Johnny Appleseed	Robert Fulton
Sam Houston		

Library of Congress Cataloging-in-Publication Data
Roberts, Russell, 1953–
    Daniel Boone / by Russell Roberts.
        p. cm. — (A Robbie Reader. What's so great about . . . ?)
    Includes bibliographical references and index. 3755 7377 5/08
    ISBN 1-58415-475-6 (lib. bound : alk. paper)
    1. Boone, Daniel, 1734–1820—Juvenile literature. 2. Pioneers—Kentucky—Biography—Juvenile literature. 3. Explorers—Kentucky—Biography—Juvenile literature. 4. Frontier and pioneer life—Kentucky—Juvenile literature. 5. Kentucky—Biography—Juvenile literature. 6. Kentucky—Discovery and exploration—Juvenile literature. I. Title. II. Series.
    F454.B66R63 2006
    976.9′02092—dc22
                                                                            2005028493

ISBN-10: 1-58415-475-6   ISBN-13: 978-1-58415-475-4

ABOUT THE AUTHOR: Russell Roberts has written and published nearly 40 books for adults and children on a variety of subjects, including baseball, memory power, business, New Jersey history, and travel. The lives of American figures of distinction is a particular area of interest for him. He has written numerous books for Mitchell Lane, including *Pedro Menendez de Aviles, Philo Farnsworth Invents TV, Robert Goddard, Bernardo de Galvez,* and *Where Did the Dinosaurs Go?* He lives in Bordentown, New Jersey, with his family and a fat, fuzzy, and crafty calico cat named Rusti.

PHOTO CREDITS: Cover—MPI/Getty Images; pp. 1, 4, 10—Stock Montage/Getty Images; pp. 6, 7, 8, 9, 14, 18, 25—Library of Congress; pp. 20, 22, 27—Sharon Beck; pp. 24, 26—Jamie Kondrchek.

PLB

TABLE OF CONTENTS

Words in **bold** type can be found in the glossary.

Daniel Boone poses with his long rifle and a hunting dog.

Ambush

The British Army moved slowly. They were marching through a thick forest. Nervously the soldiers looked around. Behind every large tree might be an Indian. Perhaps a French soldier was hiding behind some rocks. Twigs snapped. Leaves rustled. Birds called. Each sound made the British soldiers jump.

It was July 9, 1755. England and France were fighting the French and Indian War for control of North America. Different tribes of Indians fought for either side. The Algonquin (al-GON-kwin) and Huron tribes of Indians were fighting for the French. The Iroquois and their allies were fighting for the English. But it was often hard to identify Indian tribes in battle. Indians did not wear uniforms.

Edward Braddock was a British general during the French and Indian War. He led an army of about 1,200 men in an attack on the French at Fort Duquesne (doo-KAYN). Before the British soldiers could reach the fort, they were ambushed and defeated. The attack cost Braddock his life.

The British did wear uniforms. They wore bright red coats. The French and Indians wore dull colors and hid behind trees. Edward Braddock led the British. He laughed at the thought of Indians being soldiers. He thought his men were much better.

A 21-year-old army wagon driver named Daniel Boone knew better. He knew Indians well. He knew they fought hard. Boone was one of many Americans with the British Army. Another was a soldier from Virginia. His name was George Washington.

During the French and Indian War, George Washington was an aide to General Braddock. He helped lead the remains of Braddock's army to safety after it was ambushed.

Boone guided his wagon through the forest. He had never been there before. He liked that. He liked exploring new places. He had just heard about another new place. It was called Kentucky.

7

Braddock's army was attacked by the French and Indian forces. Out in the open, red-coated troops of the British Army were easy targets for their hidden attackers.

Suddenly there were gunshots, then men were shouting. French soldiers and their Indian allies popped out of the woods like magic. Then they melted back into the forest. The confused English shot at shadows. This type of fighting was new to them.

Americans ran for cover, but the British did not. They stayed in the open. In their red coats, they were easy targets. Many died. Then Braddock was shot. The soldiers panicked.

Three years after Boone served under General Braddock, the British did capture Fort Duquesne. With this victory and several others, the British won the war. When the French signed the peace treaty, their influence in North America ended.

The British renamed it Fort Pitt, and later this area would be the site of Pittsburgh, Pennsylvania.

Bullets whizzed by Boone. He knew he must escape. He jumped onto the back of a horse. The enemy was everywhere. Would he make it?

As a young man, Daniel Boone dreamed of exploring new lands. He became a good hunter while he was still a teenager.

Young Daniel

Daniel Boone was born in Exeter Township, Pennsylvania on October 22, 1734 (see chronology on page 28). His parents were Squire and Sarah Morgan Boone. They were **Quakers.**

Daniel hated staying indoors. He loved wandering outside. When he was six, **smallpox** struck Exeter. Everyone was afraid of this terrible disease. Parents kept their children inside. Daniel was unhappy. Then he had an idea. One night he snuck to the house of a friend who was sick with smallpox. He wanted to catch the disease. When he recovered, he thought, he could again go out. He did not realize that he might not recover. He could die.

Daniel caught smallpox. Sarah could not understand how. Finally Daniel told her what he had done. She was upset, but she did not punish him. She knew how he felt. Fortunately, Daniel recovered.

When Daniel was 15, his family moved to North Carolina. They settled in the Yadkin River Valley. There were no towns or stores there yet. The roads were narrow dirt trails. A family had to hunt or grow food to survive.

Daniel became a good hunter. The Indians taught him about the forest. He learned animal noises. He learned how to move silently through the woods. He learned survival.

Daniel made money hunting. A male deer was worth a silver dollar. Since a male deer is called a buck, a dollar came to be called a buck. A dollar is still called a buck today.

Daniel was an expert shot. He carried a long rifle. It had a barrel 40 inches long. It weighed 10 pounds. People said he could shoot a tick off the nose of a bear. Daniel called his rifle Ticklicker.

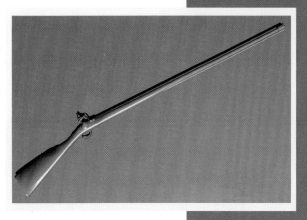

The long rifle's extremely long barrel made it more accurate than rifles before it. However, it could shoot only one shot before it needed reloading, so it was unsuitable to use against more than one threat.

Daniel and some men had a shooting contest. The men cheated. The target already had a hole in it. They pretended to shoot at it. Then Daniel shot. His bullet went through the hole. He won the contest.

In 1755 Daniel joined up with Braddock's army. There he met John Findley. Findley told him about a place called Kentucky. The grass was green and the water was sweet and pure. It had plenty of **game**. It was filled with buffalo and deer.

Daniel was excited. It sounded wonderful. He wanted to explore it. Then came that terrible battle in July. The British Army was defeated.

Fortunately, Daniel escaped.

Boone frequently encountered Indians of the Shawnee tribe during his exploits in Kentucky. The Shawnee tried desperately to keep Kentucky from being overrun by settlers.

Kentucky Bound

Daniel Boone returned to the Yadkin River Valley. There he met a girl named Rebecca Bryan. The two were married on August 14, 1756.

Daniel often left Rebecca alone to go on Long Hunts. They lasted months or even years. By herself, Rebecca raised their children. She defended their home. She grew crops. She milked cows. She could not read or write, but she was a strong, brave woman.

Daniel kept exploring. He went to Florida. During the trip, there were few animals to hunt. He almost starved.

Daniel took his son James on hunts. James was just eight years old. To keep him warm on cold nights, Daniel buttoned him inside his shirt. Daniel taught James about the forest.

Daniel explored other places. Still he thought about Kentucky. One day in 1768, Findley came to his home. He spun more magic tales of Kentucky. Boone got excited again.

In May of 1769, Boone left for Kentucky. Five other men went with him. It was a dangerous trip. The Shawnee Indians did not want any settlers in Kentucky. It was their hunting ground.

Boone and his friends reached Kentucky. It was beautiful. Wildlife was everywhere. Boone was happy. Then Indians surprised them. They took their animal skins. The Indians told them to leave and not come back. Boone stayed. Again Indians surprised him. Again they took his skins and furs. Finally he returned home. Was Kentucky worth the trouble?

Boone thought so. He thought about Kentucky often over the next few years. On September 25, 1773, he started there with his family. With him were other families. All of them wanted a new life.

The trip was a disaster. Indians angry at the settlers' return attacked them. They killed several people. They killed James Boone. Rebecca gave Daniel a special sheet to bury James. She had hoped to use it to start a new life. Now she was burying her son in it.

Everyone went back to North Carolina. They gave up their dreams.

Even then, Boone did not give up. In 1775 a man named Richard Henderson bought Kentucky land from the Cherokees for a fourteenth American colony. He called it Transylvania. He needed a road built to Kentucky. Daniel Boone would lead the builders.

Work started in March 1775. It was hard. Indians attacked them. Food was scarce. Still, they carved out a road. It was 250 miles long. It went through the Cumberland Gap, a large pass in the mountains. The trail was called Wilderness Road.

Boone rescues his daughter Jemima and another girl, who had been kidnapped by Indians. Boone got along well with many groups of Indians. They taught him skills he would use to become a superior woodsman. Relations turned sour with some groups, though, when he and other settlers moved to Kentucky.

Troubles

New settlers came to Kentucky. They built a small **community** (kuh-MYEW-nih-tee) called Boonesborough (BOONS-buh-roh) in honor of Daniel Boone. It was just a few cabins with a high fence on two sides.

Boone went home and brought his family back. Others came too. Each new family built a small cabin. The floor was dirt. There was no glass in the windows.

Food was either grown or hunted. There was no bread. Sometimes people ate meat three times a day. Although it was a hard life, more people kept coming to Kentucky.

The Indians got angry. They knew the settlers intended to stay. They attacked. In July 1776, Indians kidnapped Boone's daughter

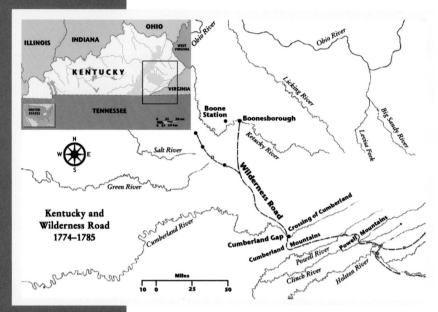

Kentucky and
Wilderness Road
1774–1785

Daniel Boone helped blaze the Wilderness Road into Kentucky. The road went through the Cumberland Gap, a natural pass through the Cumberland Mountains near the modern borders of Kentucky, Tennessee, and Virginia.

Jemima and two other girls. Boone and others tracked them. The girls secretly tore bits of cloth from their dresses. They dropped them as clues for Boone. He and the others rescued the girls, but more trouble lay ahead.

In the winter of 1778, the Shawnees captured Daniel Boone. He was a prisoner for four months. But he was clever. He pretended to like living with them. He hunted with them. He wore their clothes. He fixed their guns. He

20

laughed at their jokes. The Shawnee called him Sheltowee, which means "Big Turtle."

The trick worked. The Shawnees did not watch Boone closely. Finally he saw his chance. He escaped. On horseback and foot he raced 160 miles through the woods in just four days. Every second was precious. He had to warn everyone. The Indians planned to attack!

When he reached Boonesborough, his family was gone. They had thought he was dead, so they went home. Daniel stayed. The community needed his help.

Later that winter, hundreds of Indians (mainly Shawnees) attacked the settlers. The British helped the Shawnees. It looked hopeless. The settlers had only 50 riflemen. The Indians shot flaming arrows at the cabins. They tried to dig under the fence.

The attack failed. Boone and the settlers survived. Their success helped defeat the British in the West. This helped the American colonies win the Revolutionary War, which had begun in 1775. Not only did Boone help the settlers, he helped America too.

George Caleb Bingham painted *Daniel Boone Escorting Settlers through the Cumberland Gap* in the 1850s. It shows what these dangerous expeditions into the great wilderness of Kentucky must have been like for the settlers.

Still Wandering

Over the years, Kentucky changed. In 1792 it became the fifteenth American state. More people arrived. Game disappeared. Boone thought Kentucky was getting "too crowded."

Daniel Boone heard about a new place. It was called Missouri. In 1799 he and his family moved there. He was 65 years old. He was starting over.

For a while Missouri was fine. Then Boone lost most of his land in legal claims.

Boone wanted to fight for America once more in 1812. America was again at war with the British. The army would not let Boone

volunteer (vah-lun-TEER) because he was 78 years old.

In 1813 Rebecca died. Daniel missed her terribly. They had been married 57 years.

Still he did not settle down. He kept exploring. In 1815 he went to the Rocky Mountains. He was 81 years old.

In 1819 an artist painted Boone's portrait. It is the only painting made of Boone while he

Even in his old age, the passion to see new places never left Boone. He visited the Rocky Mountains when he was over 80 years old.

An 1820 copy of a full-length portrait of Daniel Boone that no longer exists. It is considered the first accurate picture of the typical clothes that American frontiersmen, including Boone, wore.

was alive. The artist asked if Boone had ever gotten lost on a Long Hunt.

"No," Boone joked. "But I was **bewildered** [bee-WIL-derd] once for three days."

Daniel Boone died in Missouri on September 26, 1820. His wandering was finally over . . . maybe.

There is a mystery about where Daniel Boone is buried. It has gone on a long time. Some people say Missouri. Some say Kentucky.

No one knows for sure. So maybe Boone's wandering is not yet over.

Daniel Boone is still a familiar name to many people. They know he was a pioneer and explorer who helped settle Kentucky. The Daniel Boone National Forest in Kentucky

Taken around 1950, this picture shows one of Boone's possible gravesites in Frankfort, Kentucky. He was buried in Missouri when he died in 1820. His remains were supposed to have been moved to Kentucky, but no one is certain that that's what happened. There are gravesites in both states.

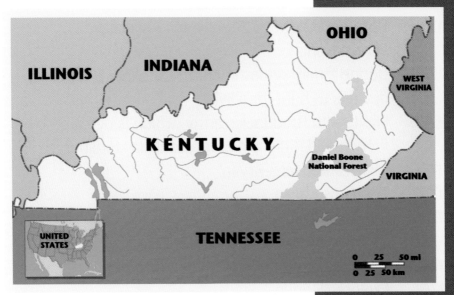

The Daniel Boone National Forest (in pale blue) stretches down the eastern side of Kentucky.

stretches across 21 counties. It contains several state parks. Naming a wilderness area after Boone is a fitting way to remember how the land was when Daniel Boone first explored it.

Because of his deeds, many people will remember the name Daniel Boone.

CHRONOLOGY

1734 Born on October 22* in Exeter Township, Pennsylvania

1749 Boone family settles in North Carolina; Boone decides to hunt for a living

1755 Fights with Braddock's army, which is defeated by French and Indians near present-day Pittsburgh

1756 Marries Rebecca Bryan

1757 Son James born

1759 Son Israel born

1760 Daughter Susannah born

1762 Daughter Jemima born

1765 Explores Florida

1766 Daughter Levina born

1768 Daughter Rebecca born

1769 In May leaves for a Kentucky Long Hunt with five others; in December is captured by Shawnee Indians; son Daniel born

1773 Son James killed by Indians; son Jesse born

1775 Son William born in June; he dies a few weeks later; Daniel leads party building Wilderness Road; founds Boonesborough

1776 Rescues Jemima Boone and other girls from Indians

1778 Captured by Shawnee Indians in February; escapes; leads successful defense of Boonesborough

1781 Son Nathan born

1782 Son Israel is killed by Indians

1799 Moves to Missouri

1813 Wife, Rebecca, dies

1820 Dies on September 26

*Some historians claim Boone's birth date was November 2, 1734. However, the author finds that the preponderance of current evidence supports the date of October 22.

TIMELINE IN HISTORY

1701	Yale is founded.
1716	First theater in American colonies is built in Williamsburg, Virginia.
1718	New Orleans is founded.
1730	Baltimore, Maryland, is settled.
1742	Franklin stove is invented by Benjamin Franklin.
1752	Benjamin Franklin conducts electricity experiment with a kite.
1758	First Indian reservation in North America is established.
1759	First music store in America is opened in Philadelphia.
1765	First chocolate is manufactured in North America in Massachusetts.
1773	Patriots throw 342 chests of tea into the harbor at the Boston Tea Party.
1775	The Revolutionary War begins at Lexington and Concord.
1781	British surrender at Yorktown, Virginia, effectively ending the Revolutionary War.
1786	Davy Crockett is born.
1789	George Washington is inaugurated as first president of the United States.
1793	Eli Whitney applies for patent for cotton gin.
1802	U.S. Military Academy at West Point is established.
1803	Louisiana Purchase doubles the size of the United States.
1812	War of 1812 begins.
1814	Washington, D.C., is captured by the British.
1832	Black Hawk War begins in Illinois.
1835	Model telegraph is built and demonstrated.
1841	*The Deerslayer* by James Fenimore Cooper is published.
1843	The great migration over the Oregon Trail begins.

FIND OUT MORE

Books

Armentrout, David, and Patricia Armentrout. *Daniel Boone.* Vero Beach, Florida: Rourke Publishers, 2001.

Greene, Carol. *Daniel Boone: Man of the Forests.* Chicago: Childrens Press, 1990.

Johnston, Marianne. *Daniel Boone.* New York: PowerKids Press, 2001.

Kozar, Richard F. *Daniel Boone and the Exploration of the Frontier.* Philadelphia: Chelsea House Publishers, 2000.

Lawlor, Laurie. *Daniel Boone.* Niles, Illinois: A. Whitman, 1989.

Nemerson, Roy. *Daniel Boone.* New York: Baronet Books, 1996.

Sanford, William R., and Carl R. Green. *Daniel Boone: Wilderness Pioneer.* Springfield, New Jersey: Enslow Publishers, Inc., 1997.

Works Consulted

Draper, Lyman C. *The Life of Daniel Boone.* Mechanicsburg, Pennsylvania: Stackpole Books, 1998.

Elliott, Lawrence. *The Long Hunter: A New Life of Daniel Boone.* New York: Reader's Digest Press, 1976.

Faragher, John Mack. *Daniel Boone.* New York: Henry Holt and Company, 1992.

On the Internet

American West: "Daniel Boone"
http://www.americanwest.com/pages/boone.htm

The Daniel Boone Homestead
http://www.berksweb.com/boone.html

McCreary's Pioneer Cemetery Preservation Society, Inc.
"Daniel Boone: The Extraordinary Life of a Common Man"
http://www.mpcps.org/boone/

Roadside America: "Boone's Bones Brouhaha"
(article about the controversy over Boone's grave)
http://www.roadsideamerica.com/set/HISTboone.html

GLOSSARY

ambush (AM-bush)—To hide and wait for an enemy, then give a surprise attack.

bewildered (bee-WIL-derd)—To be confused or puzzled.

community (kuh-MYEW-nih-tee)—A social group whose members live in a certain area and share a government.

game—Wildlife that can be hunted for food.

Quakers (KWAY-kers)—Members of the religious group the Society of Friends.

smallpox—A contagious disease that can be fatal; it often leaves the skin scarred.

volunteer (vah-lun-TEER)—To willingly step in to help.

INDEX